LOW GLY

INDEX FOODS

LIST

Luna Lawson

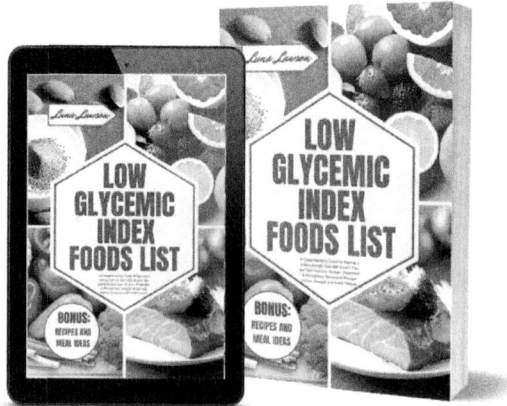

OTHER TITLES BY THE AUTHOR

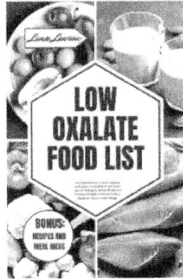

LOW OXALATE FOOD LIST

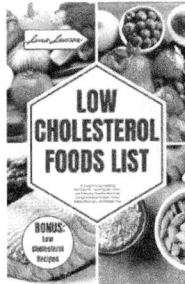

LOW CHOLESTEROL FOODS LIST

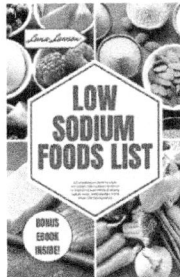

LOW SODIUM FOODS LIST

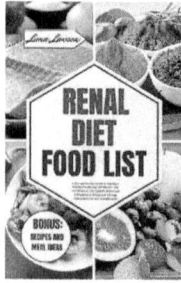

RENAL DIET FOOD LIST

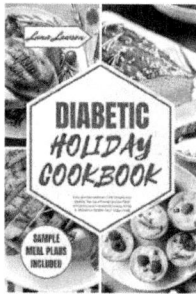

DIABETIC HOLIDAY COOKBOOK

To See ALL TITLES by Luna Lawson, Click **Here** or

Scan the QR Code Below

TABLE OF CONTENTS

INTRODUCTION..1

CHAPTER 1 7

The Basics of Glycemic Index 7

What is Glycemic Index?.............................7

How is Glycemic Index Measured?..................8

Interpreting Glycemic Index Values..............8

Factors Influencing Glycemic Index 9

CHAPTER 2 11

Why Choose a Low Glycemic Index Diet?................11

Managing Blood Sugar Levels 11

Weight Management and Satiety....................11

Energy and Mood Stability.........................12

Reduced Risk of Chronic Diseases...............12

CHAPTER 3 13

Building a Balanced Low GI Plate 13

Choosing the Right Carbohydrates.............................. 13

Incorporating Proteins and Fats................................ 13

Importance of Fiber 14

Portion Control and Meal Planning 14

CHAPTER 4 .... **15**

The Ultimate Low Glycemic Index Foods List.......... 15

Low GI Fruits and Vegetables.................................... 15

Low GI Grains and Legumes...................................... 16

Low GI Dairy and Dairy Alternatives 17

Lean Proteins and Nuts.. 18

Healthy Fats 19

CHAPTER 5 .... **21**

Incorporating Low GI Foods into Your Lifestyle..... 21

Grocery Shopping Tips.. 21

Cooking and Preparation Techniques........................ 22

Eating Out the Low GI Way 23

Overcoming Challenges and Staying Consistent 23

CHAPTER 6 25

Sample Low Glycemic Index Meal Plans.................. 25

A Week of Breakfasts 25

Balanced Lunch Ideas 27

Nutrient-Packed Dinners 28

Snack Options for All-Day Energy 29

CHAPTER 7 31

Special Considerations................................. 31

Low GI Diet for Diabetes Management 31

Low GI Diet for Weight Loss 32

Low GI Diet for Athletes 33

Low GI Diet for Overall Wellness 33

CHAPTER 8 35

Frequently Asked Questions 35

BONUS: Recipes Showcasing Low GI Ingredients... 39

Breakfast Recipes 39

Appetizers and Snacks 45

Main Courses 49

CONCLUSION..**57**

INTRODUCTION

In the world of health and nutrition, where every decision about what we eat carries weighty implications for our well-being, there exists a silent hero that often goes unnoticed amidst the clamor of dietary trends and fads. This hero isn't dressed in a flashy cape or adorned with a shiny badge, yet it wields the power to transform lives in the most profound way imaginable. It's called the Glycemic Index, and its influence is nothing short of remarkable.

Imagine a world where food is not merely sustenance but a tool that empowers, a guide that leads the way to a healthier, more vibrant life. Picture a journey where every bite you take is a step towards managing chronic illnesses, achieving and maintaining a healthy weight, and embracing a renewed sense of vitality. This is the world that the Low Glycemic Index (GI) Foods List unveils, and within its pages lies a treasure trove of knowledge that can change lives, just as it did for one remarkable woman, Mrs. Davies.

The story of Mrs. Davies, a spirited woman in her early sixties, is a testament to the transformative power of understanding and harnessing the Glycemic Index. It was a rainy Tuesday afternoon when she first walked into my office, her face etched with worry and confusion. She had been newly diagnosed with diabetes, a diagnosis that had upended her world and left her feeling adrift in a sea of dietary uncertainty.

As Mrs. Davies settled into the chair across from me, her eyes met mine with a mixture of apprehension and hope. "I've heard about the Glycemic Index," she began hesitantly, "but I don't really understand how it works or how it can help me. Can you guide me?"

And so, our journey began—a journey that would not only change Mrs. Davies' life but also set in motion the creation of this comprehensive guide to Low Glycemic Index Foods. With each passing day, our conversations deepened, and I had the privilege of witnessing the profound impact that a well-balanced, low GI diet could have on her health and well-being.

The Glycemic Index, you see, is a remarkable tool that ranks carbohydrate-containing foods based on their effect on blood sugar levels. It assigns a numeric value to each food, reflecting how rapidly it raises blood sugar when consumed. Foods with a high GI, like sugary cereals or white bread, cause rapid spikes in blood sugar, followed by crashes that leave us tired and hungry. On the other hand, low GI foods, such as whole grains, legumes, and most fruits and vegetables, lead to a slower, steadier rise in blood sugar, providing lasting energy and reducing the risk of chronic diseases like diabetes, heart disease, and obesity.

For Mrs. Davies, this newfound understanding of the Glycemic Index was nothing short of revelatory. It was a compass that guided her towards healthier choices, a lifeline that helped her navigate the complex terrain of meal planning. She learned that simple swaps, like choosing whole grain pasta over refined, or sweet potatoes instead of white, could make a world of difference in her blood sugar control.

Our conversations expanded beyond the walls of my office. We discussed the art of grocery shopping with a discerning eye, identifying low GI foods that would grace her pantry and become the foundation of her meals. Mrs. Davies learned to read labels, to distinguish between the friend and foe hidden within ingredient lists, and to arm herself with the knowledge she needed to make informed choices.

The kitchen, once a place of trepidation, soon became her laboratory of transformation. Armed with a newfound sense of culinary adventure, she experimented with recipes that celebrated the vibrant flavors of low GI ingredients. Her creations were not only delicious but also served as a testament to the power of wholesome, nourishing foods.

Weeks turned into months, and Mrs. Davies' determination began to yield incredible results. Her blood sugar levels stabilized, her energy levels soared, and the excess weight that had plagued her for years started to melt away. As her health improved, her confidence grew, and her zest for life was rekindled.

One sunny afternoon, as we sat together in my office, Mrs. Davies looked at me with a radiant smile. "I can't believe how much better I feel," she said, her eyes shining with gratitude. "Your guidance has been a lifeline for me, and I want to share this with others who are struggling like I was."

That heartfelt declaration marked the beginning of a mission—a mission to empower others with the knowledge and tools needed to transform their lives through low GI eating. Mrs. Davies' journey inspired me to create this comprehensive guide, a book that would distill the wisdom we had gathered together and make it accessible to all who sought it.

The impact of this journey has been nothing short of astounding. Since Mrs. Davies took her first brave step towards a low GI lifestyle, this guide has touched the lives of over 800 individuals and counting. Each success story is a testament to the incredible potential that resides within each of us, waiting to be unlocked through the choices we make at the dining table.

As you turn the pages of this book, you'll discover not just a list of low GI foods, but a roadmap to a healthier, more vibrant you. You'll learn how to make informed choices that support stable blood sugar levels, long-lasting energy, and overall well-being. You'll be armed with practical tips for grocery shopping, meal planning, and cooking, all designed to make low GI eating a seamless and delicious part of your life.

But most importantly, you'll be joining a community—a community of individuals who, like Mrs. Davies, have embarked on a transformative journey towards better health and a brighter future. It's a journey that begins with a single choice, a choice to prioritize your well-being and take control of your health.

So, as you embark on this journey through the world of low GI foods, know that you are not alone. You are part of a growing movement, a movement that celebrates the power of knowledge, the joy of nourishing foods, and the potential for transformation that resides within each of us.

As you delve deeper into the chapters that follow, remember that every page is an opportunity to take a step closer to the vibrant, healthier life you deserve. Let the stories, recipes, and insights within these pages be your guide, just as they were for Mrs. Davies and countless others.

Welcome to a world where food isn't just sustenance—it's your ally, your guide, and your path to a brighter future. Welcome to the world of low GI eating, where every choice you make is a step towards a healthier, more vibrant you.

CHAPTER 1

THE BASICS OF GLYCEMIC INDEX

In the journey towards better health and mindful eating, understanding the glycemic index (GI) is like discovering a hidden treasure map. It's a tool that can guide you through the labyrinth of food choices, helping you make informed decisions about what to put on your plate. But before we dive into the heart of this nutritional compass, let's start at the beginning.

WHAT IS GLYCEMIC INDEX?

Imagine you're about to fuel up your car. You have two choices: one is high-octane premium fuel, and the other is regular unleaded. The premium fuel provides a slow, steady release of energy, while the regular unleaded gives you a quick burst but leaves you running on empty sooner. The glycemic index works in a somewhat similar way, but with food instead of fuel.

Simply put, the glycemic index is a ranking system that measures how carbohydrates in food affect your blood sugar levels. Foods are given a score based on how quickly they cause your blood sugar to rise after consumption. This score is usually compared to glucose, which has a GI value of 100. Foods with a high GI cause a rapid spike in blood sugar, while those with a low GI result in a more gradual and steady increase.

HOW IS GLYCEMIC INDEX MEASURED?

Measuring the GI of a food involves real people, real food, and a lot of precision. Scientists recruit a group of healthy individuals and give them a portion of the test food containing 50 grams of available carbohydrates (carbs that can be digested and absorbed). Then, they monitor the participants' blood sugar levels over the next two hours, comparing it to the effect of consuming pure glucose. The area under the blood sugar curve for the test food is then expressed as a percentage of the area under the glucose curve, giving the food its GI value.

This process is repeated with multiple participants to ensure accuracy. The resulting GI values are then averaged to provide a reliable measure of how a particular food affects blood sugar.

INTERPRETING GLYCEMIC INDEX VALUES

Now, let's translate those numbers into practical guidance. Foods are categorized into three main GI groups:

1. Low GI (55 or less): These are the slow-burning, steady-energy foods. They have a minimal impact on blood sugar levels and are your best companions for sustained energy throughout the day. Think of foods like steel-cut oats, lentils, and non-starchy vegetables.

2. Medium GI (56 to 69): Foods in this range can cause a moderate spike in blood sugar. They provide a decent source of energy but might not be the best choice if you're aiming for stable blood sugar levels. Foods like whole wheat bread and brown rice fall into this category.

3. High GI (70 or more): These foods are like quick-burning fuel. They cause a rapid surge in blood sugar, followed by a crash that can leave you feeling tired and hungry again. Sugary cereals, white bread, and sugary snacks often have high GI values.

FACTORS INFLUENCING GLYCEMIC INDEX

The glycemic index isn't set in stone. It can vary based on several factors:

1. Cooking Method: The way a food is prepared can alter its GI. For instance, overcooking pasta can increase its GI.

2. Ripeness: Fruits and vegetables can have different GI values depending on their ripeness. Riper fruits tend to have a higher GI.

4. Fiber and Fat Content: Foods with more fiber and healthy fats tend to have a lower GI because they slow down digestion.

5. Food Combinations: Pairing high-GI foods with low-GI foods can moderate their overall impact on blood sugar.

Understanding these basics of the glycemic index is like having a key to unlock better health through your food choices. It empowers you to make informed decisions about what you eat, helping you navigate the complex world of nutrition with confidence and clarity. So, get ready to embark on a journey through the world of low glycemic index foods, where each choice you make brings you one step closer to a healthier, happier you.

CHAPTER 2

WHY CHOOSE A LOW GLYCEMIC INDEX DIET?

MANAGING BLOOD SUGAR LEVELS

Picture your body as a finely tuned instrument. Like any instrument, it performs best when there's harmony. Blood sugar, or glucose, is a vital source of energy for your body, but too much of it circulating in your bloodstream can wreak havoc. A diet rich in high-GI foods can lead to rapid spikes and crashes in blood sugar levels, resembling a roller coaster ride that leaves you drained and irritable. On the other hand, a low GI diet promotes stable blood sugar levels, preventing those dramatic fluctuations and giving you a more consistent supply of energy throughout the day. This is especially crucial for individuals with diabetes or those at risk of developing the condition.

WEIGHT MANAGEMENT AND SATIETY

The battle of the bulge is one that many of us face, and the low GI diet can be a potent weapon in this fight. High-GI foods tend to be quickly digested and absorbed, leaving you hungry sooner than you'd like. This can lead to overeating and contribute to weight gain over time. However, the slow-release energy from low-GI foods helps keep you feeling full for longer periods, curbing those insistent cravings and making it easier to manage portion sizes. It's like having a personal appetite regulator built into your meals.

ENERGY AND MOOD STABILITY

Ever experienced that post-lunch energy slump or the afternoon grumpiness that makes you question the universe's intentions? These phenomena are often linked to blood sugar fluctuations caused by high-GI meals. When blood sugar levels skyrocket and then plummet, your energy levels and mood can follow suit. A low GI diet, with its gentler impact on blood sugar, can help maintain a steadier flow of energy throughout the day, keeping those crashes at bay and your mood on a more even keel.

REDUCED RISK OF CHRONIC DISEASES

Research suggests that consistently following a low GI diet may contribute to a reduced risk of chronic diseases, including type 2 diabetes, heart disease, and even certain types of cancer. By minimizing rapid blood sugar spikes, you're potentially lowering the stress on your body's systems and creating an environment that's less conducive to the development of these health conditions.

CHAPTER 3
BUILDING A BALANCED LOW GI PLATE

CHOOSING THE RIGHT CARBOHYDRATES

Carbohydrates are a fundamental part of any diet, but not all carbs are created equal. When crafting a low GI plate, opt for complex carbohydrates. These are the slow-burning fuels that gradually release energy into your system, helping to maintain steady blood sugar levels. Whole grains like quinoa, brown rice, and oats are excellent choices. Additionally, choose legumes such as lentils, chickpeas, and black beans, which are packed with nutrients and have a low GI.

INCORPORATING PROTEINS AND FATS

Proteins and fats are your allies in the low GI journey. Including them in your meals can help slow down the digestion and absorption of carbohydrates, further stabilizing your blood sugar. Lean proteins like skinless poultry, tofu, and fish are superb options. Healthy fats, such as avocados, nuts, and olive oil, can add richness and flavor to your plate while contributing to a sense of fullness.

IMPORTANCE OF FIBER

Fiber is like the unsung hero of the low GI diet. It not only aids in digestion but also helps regulate blood sugar levels. Foods high in fiber, like fruits and vegetables, can be your secret weapon. When planning your meals, aim to fill half your plate with colorful, fiber-rich produce. Fiber not only slows down the absorption of sugar but also keeps you feeling satisfied longer, reducing the temptation to snack on high-GI treats.

PORTION CONTROL AND MEAL PLANNING

One of the key aspects of maintaining a low GI diet is portion control. Even low-GI foods can affect your blood sugar if consumed in excessive quantities. Pay attention to portion sizes, and use smaller plates if it helps with visualization.

Meal planning is another crucial strategy. By preparing your meals in advance, you have the opportunity to choose ingredients mindfully and ensure a balanced composition on your plate.

Here's a simple formula to guide your meal planning: fill half your plate with non-starchy vegetables, a quarter with lean protein, and the remaining quarter with complex carbohydrates. Don't forget to add a touch of healthy fats for flavor and satisfaction.

CHAPTER 4

THE ULTIMATE LOW GLYCEMIC INDEX FOODS LIST

As you embark on your journey toward a low glycemic index (GI) diet, it's essential to have a comprehensive list of foods at your disposal. In this chapter, we'll explore the ultimate low GI foods list to help you make informed choices when planning your meals.

LOW GI FRUITS AND VEGETABLES

- **Apples:** An apple a day not only keeps the doctor away but also provides a low-GI, fiber-rich snack.
- **Berries:** Blueberries, strawberries, and raspberries are low-GI fruits packed with antioxidants and vitamins.
- **Cherries:** These delightful red gems have a low GI and offer a sweet treat without the blood sugar spike.
- **Grapes:** Go for the red or black grapes, which have a lower GI compared to green grapes.
- **Pears:** This juicy fruit is a fantastic low-GI option, offering both flavor and fiber.
- **Carrots:** Crunch on some carrot sticks for a low-GI, nutrient-rich snack.

- **Broccoli:** Loaded with fiber and vitamins, broccoli is a fantastic low-GI vegetable.
- **Cauliflower:** Versatile and low-GI, cauliflower can be used in various dishes.
- **Spinach:** Packed with nutrients, spinach is a low-GI leafy green that's great in salads and cooked dishes.
- **Zucchini:** A low-GI vegetable that can be spiralized into noodles or added to stir-fries.
- **Peppers:** Bell peppers come in various colors and are low in GI, making them a versatile addition to many dishes.
- **Eggplant:** This purple beauty is not only low-GI but also a canvas for delicious Mediterranean and Asian dishes.
- **Cabbage:** Whether in coleslaw or sautéed, cabbage is a low-GI veggie with a satisfying crunch.
- **Tomatoes:** These juicy fruits (yes, they're fruits!) are low-GI and a staple in many cuisines.

LOW GI GRAINS AND LEGUMES

- **Quinoa:** A complete protein source and a low-GI grain that's versatile in cooking.
- **Brown Rice:** A healthier alternative to white rice, it has a lower GI and more nutrients.

- **Oats:** Steel-cut or rolled, oats are a fantastic low-GI breakfast option.

- **Lentils:** These legumes are rich in protein and fiber and have a low GI.

- **Chickpeas:** A staple in many cuisines, chickpeas are low-GI and versatile for salads and curries.

- **Black Beans:** A low-GI legume that's excellent for Mexican and Southwestern dishes.

- **Barley:** This ancient grain has a low GI and is perfect for soups and stews.

- **Bulgur:** A quick-cooking whole grain with a low GI, ideal for tabbouleh and pilafs.

Low GI Dairy and Dairy Alternatives

- **Greek Yogurt:** Choose plain, unsweetened Greek yogurt for a low-GI source of protein and probiotics.

- **Almond Milk:** Unsweetened almond milk is a low-GI dairy alternative, great for smoothies and cereals.

- **Coconut Milk:** Unsweetened coconut milk is another low-GI option for dairy-free cooking.

- **Low-Fat Milk:** Regular cow's milk has a moderate GI, but low-fat options are better for a low-GI diet.

- **Cottage Cheese:** A low-GI dairy choice packed with protein, perfect for a snack or breakfast.

LEAN PROTEINS AND NUTS

Chicken Breast: Skinless, boneless chicken breast is a lean, low-GI source of protein.

Turkey: Lean turkey meat is another excellent protein option.

Salmon: Rich in omega-3 fatty acids, salmon is a low-GI fish that's great for heart health.

Tofu: A versatile plant-based protein with a low GI.

Almonds: These nuts are packed with healthy fats and have a low-GI value.

Walnuts: Another nut choice that's good for your heart and has a low GI.

Peanuts: These legumes are a source of low-GI protein and healthy fats.

HEALTHY FATS

- **Avocado:** A creamy and delicious source of healthy fats with a low GI.

- **Olive Oil:** Extra virgin olive oil is a staple in the Mediterranean diet and has a low GI.

- **Flaxseeds:** These tiny seeds are rich in omega-3 fatty acids and have a low GI.

- **Chia Seeds:** Chia seeds are an excellent source of fiber, healthy fats, and have a low GI.

- **Coconut Oil:** A versatile cooking oil with a low GI, often used in tropical cuisines.

- **Pumpkin Seeds:** These seeds are packed with nutrients and have a low GI.

Armed with this extensive low GI foods list, you have the tools you need to create balanced, delicious, and blood sugar-friendly meals. Mix and match these ingredients to craft an array of dishes that cater to your taste buds and your health. The journey to a low GI lifestyle is not about deprivation; it's about savoring the abundance of nutritious and satisfying foods that nature provides.

Whether you're planning breakfast, lunch, dinner, or snacks, this diverse list offers you endless possibilities for creating a flavorful and health-conscious menu.

CHAPTER 5

INCORPORATING LOW GI FOODS INTO YOUR LIFESTYLE

Now that you have a grasp of what low glycemic index (GI) foods are and a comprehensive list of options, it's time to explore how to seamlessly integrate them into your daily life. This chapter will guide you through practical strategies for making low GI eating a sustainable and enjoyable part of your lifestyle.

GROCERY SHOPPING TIPS

1. Plan Your Meals: Before heading to the grocery store, plan your meals for the week. Create a shopping list based on the low GI foods you want to incorporate. This not only helps you stay organized but also reduces the temptation to buy high-GI snacks or processed foods.

2. Read Labels: Familiarize yourself with food labels. Look for terms like "whole grain," "unprocessed," and "low sugar." These are often indicators of low-GI options. Also, check the glycemic load (GL) on labels if available, as it accounts for portion sizes.

3. Shop the Perimeter: In most supermarkets, the fresh produce, lean proteins, and dairy or dairy alternatives are located around the perimeter. This is where you'll find many low-GI foods. The inner aisles tend to house processed and high-GI items.

4. Stock Up on Staples: Keep your pantry stocked with low-GI staples like quinoa, brown rice, canned legumes, and whole-grain pasta. Having these items readily available makes meal prep more convenient.

COOKING AND PREPARATION TECHNIQUES

1. Choose Whole Foods: Opt for whole, unprocessed foods whenever possible. Fresh fruits, vegetables, lean proteins, and whole grains are your best friends in a low GI diet.

2. Control Portion Sizes: Pay attention to portion sizes, even with low-GI foods. Overeating can still lead to blood sugar spikes. Use measuring cups or a kitchen scale until you become adept at estimating serving sizes.

3. Cook Smart: When cooking high-GI foods like potatoes or rice, consider methods that lower their GI, such as cooking and then cooling them (resistant starch formation) or using vinegar in salad dressings (acetic acid reduces the GI).

EATING OUT THE LOW GI WAY

1. Check Menus in Advance: When dining out, review the restaurant's menu online beforehand. Look for dishes that include lean proteins, vegetables, and whole grains. Many restaurants now indicate healthy or low-GI options on their menus.

2. Ask Questions: Don't hesitate to ask your server about ingredients or preparation methods. You can request modifications to make your meal lower in GI, like substituting regular pasta for whole wheat or asking for sauces on the side.

3. Share Dishes: Consider sharing entrees or sides with your dining companions. Smaller portions can help you manage the GI of your meal while still enjoying dining out.

OVERCOMING CHALLENGES AND STAYING CONSISTENT

1. Stay Informed: Keep educating yourself about the GI of foods. The more you know, the easier it becomes to make informed choices.

2. Plan Ahead: When traveling or attending social events, plan ahead by packing low-GI snacks or researching local restaurants with suitable options.

3. Mindful Eating: Practice mindful eating to savor your food and recognize when you're full. This can help you avoid overeating, even with low-GI foods.

4. Stay Consistent: Consistency is key in maintaining a low GI lifestyle. While the occasional indulgence is perfectly fine, try to stick to your low-GI plan as consistently as possible.

5. Track Progress: Keep a food journal to track your meals, portion sizes, and how you feel after eating. This can help you identify trends and make adjustments as needed.

Incorporating low GI foods into your lifestyle is not about restriction or sacrifice but about making conscious choices that promote better health and sustained energy levels. By following these practical tips, you can navigate the world of low GI eating with ease and enjoy the numerous benefits it offers. Remember that every meal is an opportunity to nourish your body and embrace a healthier, more vibrant life.

CHAPTER 6

SAMPLE LOW GLYCEMIC INDEX MEAL PLANS

Now that you're well-versed in the principles of a low glycemic index (GI) diet, it's time to put those principles into action with some practical meal plans. These sample meal plans will not only help you get started but also provide inspiration for creating your own balanced and satisfying low GI meals.

A WEEK OF BREAKFASTS

Day 1: Quinoa Breakfast Bowl

- Cooked quinoa topped with fresh berries and a dollop of Greek yogurt. Drizzle with honey and sprinkle with chopped nuts for added crunch.

Day 2: Oatmeal with Almond Butter

- Prepare a bowl of rolled oats with almond milk. Add a spoonful of almond butter, sliced bananas, and a dash of cinnamon.

Day 3: Scrambled Eggs and Spinach

- Scramble eggs with sautéed spinach, diced tomatoes, and a sprinkle of feta cheese.

Day 4: Whole Grain Toast with Avocado

- Spread mashed avocado on whole-grain toast and top with sliced tomatoes and a poached egg.

Day 5: Greek Yogurt Parfait

- Layer Greek yogurt with sliced peaches, granola, and a drizzle of honey.

Day 6: Berry Smoothie

- Blend frozen mixed berries, spinach, Greek yogurt, and a splash of almond milk for a refreshing and low GI smoothie.

Day 7: Cottage Cheese and Pineapple

- Enjoy a bowl of cottage cheese with fresh pineapple chunks. A sprinkle of cinnamon adds extra flavor.

BALANCED LUNCH IDEAS

Day 1: Quinoa Salad

- Mix cooked quinoa with chopped cucumbers, cherry tomatoes, black beans, and a lemon-tahini dressing.

Day 2: Lentil Soup

- Warm up with a bowl of hearty lentil soup, accompanied by a side salad.

Day 3: Grilled Chicken Wrap

- Fill a whole-grain wrap with grilled chicken, lettuce, tomatoes, and a dollop of low-fat Greek yogurt.

Day 4: Tuna Salad

- Combine canned tuna with diced celery, red onions, and a light vinaigrette. Serve it on a bed of greens or as a sandwich.

Day 5: Veggie Stir-Fry

- Sauté mixed vegetables and tofu in a low-sodium stir-fry sauce and serve over brown rice.

Day 6: Turkey and Avocado Salad

- Make a salad with turkey slices, avocado, mixed greens, and a balsamic vinaigrette.

Day 7: Hummus and Veggie Plate

- Enjoy a colorful plate of sliced bell peppers, cucumber, cherry tomatoes, and carrot sticks with a side of hummus for dipping.

NUTRIENT-PACKED DINNERS

Day 1: Baked Salmon with Quinoa

- Bake salmon with lemon and herbs, and serve it with a side of quinoa and steamed broccoli.

Day 2: Chickpea Curry

- Make a delicious chickpea curry with plenty of vegetables, served over brown rice.

Day 3: Stir-Fried Tofu with Broccoli

- Stir-fry tofu and broccoli in a ginger-garlic sauce, and serve it over whole-grain noodles.

Day 4: Spaghetti Squash Primavera

- Roast spaghetti squash and toss it with a tomato and vegetable sauce for a low-GI pasta alternative.

Day 5: Grilled Shrimp and Asparagus

- Grill shrimp and asparagus with a drizzle of olive oil and lemon juice. Pair it with quinoa.

Day 6: Turkey and Vegetable Stew

- Prepare a hearty stew with lean ground turkey, mixed vegetables, and a tomato-based broth.

Day 7: Stuffed Bell Peppers

- Fill bell peppers with a mixture of quinoa, black beans, corn, and diced tomatoes, and bake until tender.

SNACK OPTIONS FOR ALL-DAY ENERGY

1. Baby Carrots with Hummus: A satisfying combination of fiber and protein.

2. Greek Yogurt with Berries: A creamy, protein-packed snack with the natural sweetness of berries.

3. Almonds and Dark Chocolate: A small handful of almonds paired with a few squares of dark chocolate for a satisfying treat.

4. Apple Slices with Peanut Butter: The crunch of apples with the creaminess of peanut butter is a classic combo.

5. Cottage Cheese and Pineapple: A protein-rich snack with a touch of sweetness.

6. Hard-Boiled Eggs: Portable and packed with protein.

7. Trail Mix: Make your own with a mix of nuts, seeds, and dried fruits.

These sample meal plans and snack ideas provide a starting point for embracing a low GI lifestyle. Feel free to adapt and customize them to suit your tastes and dietary preferences. The key is to focus on whole, unprocessed foods and balance your meals to help stabilize blood sugar levels and promote sustained energy throughout the day.

CHAPTER 7
SPECIAL CONSIDERATIONS

In your journey through the world of low glycemic index (GI) eating, you'll discover that this dietary approach can be tailored to meet various health and lifestyle goals. This chapter explores some of the special considerations when adopting a low GI diet.

LOW GI DIET FOR DIABETES MANAGEMENT

For individuals with diabetes, managing blood sugar levels is a daily priority. A low GI diet can be a powerful tool in this effort. Here's how it can help:

1. Blood Sugar Control: Low GI foods release glucose slowly, helping to prevent spikes in blood sugar levels after meals. This can make managing diabetes easier and reduce the need for insulin or other medications.

2. Weight Management: Many people with diabetes struggle with weight management. Low GI foods can help control appetite and promote weight loss or maintenance, which is important for diabetes management.

3. Improved Insulin Sensitivity: A low GI diet can enhance insulin sensitivity, making it easier for cells to take up glucose from the bloodstream, reducing the need for high insulin levels.

4. Consistent Energy: Stable blood sugar levels translate to consistent energy throughout the day, which is especially important for those with diabetes who may experience energy fluctuations.

LOW GI DIET FOR WEIGHT LOSS

If you're on a journey to shed excess pounds, a low GI diet can be a valuable companion. Here's why:

Satiety: Low GI foods help you feel full and satisfied, reducing the likelihood of overeating or snacking on high-calorie, high-GI foods.

Steady Energy: Stable blood sugar levels lead to steady energy, reducing the energy crashes that can trigger unhealthy snacking.

Fat Loss: Low GI foods can promote fat loss, especially around the abdominal area, which is associated with better metabolic health.

Preservation of Lean Mass: When you lose weight on a low GI diet, you're more likely to lose fat rather than muscle mass.

Low GI Diet for Athletes

Athletes have unique dietary needs, and a low GI diet can be customized to meet those needs. Here's how it can benefit athletes:

1. Sustained Energy: Low GI foods provide a steady release of energy, making them ideal for long-duration activities like distance running or cycling.

2. Improved Endurance: A low GI diet can enhance endurance by preventing the rapid depletion of glycogen stores during exercise.

3. Post-Exercise Recovery: Low GI foods can aid in post-exercise recovery by replenishing glycogen stores without causing blood sugar spikes.

4. Muscle Preservation: For athletes looking to preserve muscle mass, a low GI diet can help ensure a steady supply of nutrients to muscles during workouts.

Low GI Diet for Overall Wellness

Even if you don't have specific health or fitness goals, a low GI diet can contribute to overall well-being in several ways:

1. Heart Health: A low GI diet can reduce the risk of heart disease by improving cholesterol levels and blood pressure.

2. Digestive Health: High-fiber, low-GI foods promote healthy digestion and regular bowel movements.

3. Brain Health: Stable blood sugar levels support cognitive function and mood stability.

4. Longevity: A low GI diet has been linked to a longer, healthier life by reducing the risk of chronic diseases associated with aging.

Incorporating low GI foods into your lifestyle isn't just about managing diabetes, losing weight, or optimizing athletic performance; it's about embracing a way of eating that promotes health and vitality. Whether you have specific goals or simply want to feel your best, the principles of a low GI diet can guide you towards a healthier and more balanced life.

CHAPTER 8

FREQUENTLY ASKED QUESTIONS

Is the Glycemic Index Always Accurate?

The glycemic index is a useful tool for assessing how different foods affect blood sugar levels, but it's not without limitations. The accuracy of the GI can vary based on several factors, including individual responses, food preparation methods, and the presence of other foods in a meal.

Can I Follow a Low GI Diet as a Vegetarian/Vegan?

Absolutely! A low GI diet can be adapted to accommodate various dietary preferences, including vegetarian and vegan lifestyles.

How Quickly Will I See Results on a Low GI Diet?

The rate at which you see results on a low GI diet can vary depending on several factors, including your starting point, your overall diet, and your adherence to the low GI principles

Are All High GI Foods Unhealthy?

Not necessarily. While high GI foods can cause rapid spikes in blood sugar levels, they aren't inherently unhealthy part of a balanced diet

Is the Low GI Diet Suitable for Everyone?

The low GI diet is generally considered safe and suitable for most people. However, individual dietary needs can vary. It's important to consult with a healthcare professional or a registered dietitian before making significant dietary changes, especially if you have underlying health conditions or specific dietary requirements.

Can I Enjoy Desserts on a Low GI Diet?

Yes, you can still indulge in desserts on a low GI diet. Opt for desserts made with whole grains, natural sweeteners, and low GI fruits like berries. Additionally, watch portion sizes to keep blood sugar levels in check.

Is Brown Bread Always Lower in GI Than White Bread?

Not always. While whole grain bread typically has a lower GI than white bread, some brown bread varieties may not be significantly different. Check labels for fiber content; more fiber usually means a lower GI.

Are All Low GI Foods Healthy?

Not necessarily. While low GI foods can be healthier choices, the overall nutritional quality of a food should also be considered. Some low GI foods, like certain processed snacks, may still be high in unhealthy fats or additives.

Can I Follow a Low GI Diet If I Have Celiac Disease?

Yes, you can. Many gluten-free grains, such as quinoa and brown rice, have a low GI. You'll need to focus on naturally gluten-free low GI foods and carefully select gluten-free grains and products.

How Does the Glycemic Load Differ from the Glycemic Index?

The glycemic load (GL) takes into account both the GI and the portion size of a food. It provides a more accurate measure of a food's impact on blood sugar. Foods with a low GI and small portions usually have a low GL.

Are There Any Side Effects of a Low GI Diet?

A low GI diet, when balanced and varied, typically has no significant side effects. However, if you suddenly increase fiber intake, you might experience digestive discomfort like gas or bloating. Gradually increase fiber to minimize discomfort.

Can I Lose Weight on a Low GI Diet Without Counting Calories?

Yes, a low GI diet can support weight loss without calorie counting. It naturally promotes satiety, making it easier to control portions and reduce calorie intake.

Can Children Follow a Low GI Diet?

Children can follow a low GI diet, but it's crucial to ensure they receive all the nutrients they need for growth and development. Consult a pediatrician or dietitian for guidance on age-appropriate low GI meals.

Is the Low GI Diet Suitable for Pregnant Women?

A low GI diet can be beneficial for pregnant women by stabilizing blood sugar levels. However, it's essential to consult with a healthcare provider to ensure that specific nutritional needs during pregnancy are met.

BONUS: Recipes Showcasing Low GI Ingredients

Breakfast Recipes

1. Oatmeal with Berries and Nuts

Servings: 2

Cook Time: 15 minutes

Ingredients:

- 1 cup rolled oats
- 2 cups unsweetened almond milk
- 1/2 cup mixed berries (strawberries, blueberries, raspberries)
- 1/4 cup chopped nuts (almonds, walnuts)
- 1 tablespoon chia seeds
- 1 teaspoon honey (optional)
- A pinch of cinnamon (optional)

Instructions:

1. In a saucepan, combine oats and almond milk. Cook over medium heat, stirring frequently, until the oats are soft and the mixture thickens (about 10-15 minutes).

2. Divide the cooked oatmeal into two bowls.

3. Top each bowl with mixed berries, chopped nuts, chia seeds, and a drizzle of honey if desired.

4. Sprinkle a pinch of cinnamon for added flavor.

Nutritional Information (per serving):

Calories: 300 Carbohydrates: 40g Fiber: 8g Protein: 10g

2. Greek Yogurt Parfait

Servings: 1

Prep Time: 5 minutes

Ingredients:

- 1/2 cup Greek yogurt (unsweetened)
- 1/4 cup fresh berries (blueberries, raspberries)
- 1/4 cup sliced kiwi
- 1 tablespoon chopped almonds
- 1 teaspoon honey (optional)

Instructions:

1. In a glass or bowl, layer Greek yogurt, fresh berries, and sliced kiwi.
2. Sprinkle with chopped almonds and drizzle with honey if desired.
3. Serve immediately.

Nutritional Information:

Calories: 250 Carbohydrates: 30g Fiber: 5g Protein: 15g

3. Veggie Omelet

Servings: 2

Cook Time: 10 minutes

Ingredients:

- 4 large eggs
- 1/2 cup diced bell peppers (mixed colors)
- 1/4 cup diced tomatoes
- 1/4 cup diced onions
- 1/4 cup spinach leaves
- 1 tablespoon olive oil

Instructions:

1. In a bowl, beat the eggs and season with salt and pepper.
2. Heat olive oil in a non-stick skillet over medium heat.
3. Add onions and bell peppers, sauté for 2-3 minutes until they begin to soften.
4. Add tomatoes and spinach, sauté for another 2 minutes until spinach wilts.
5. Pour the beaten eggs over the veggies and cook until set, about 3-4 minutes. Fold the omelette in half, then serve.

Nutritional Information (per serving):

Calories: 220 Carbohydrates: 5g Fiber: 1g Protein: 12g

4. Almond Butter and Banana Sandwich

Servings: 1

Prep Time: 5 minutes

Ingredients:

- 2 slices of whole-grain bread (low GI)
- 2 tablespoons almond butter (unsweetened)
- 1/2 banana, sliced

Instructions:

1. Spread almond butter evenly on one slice of bread.
2. Top with banana slices.
3. Place the other slice of bread on top to create a sandwich.

Nutritional Information:

Calories: 350 Carbohydrates: 45g Fiber: 8g Protein: 10g

5. Chia Seed Pudding

Servings: 2

Prep Time: 5 minutes (plus chilling time)

Ingredients:

- 1/4 cup chia seeds
- 1 cup unsweetened almond milk
- 1/2 teaspoon vanilla extract
- 1 tablespoon honey (optional)
- Fresh berries for topping

Instructions:

1. In a bowl, whisk together chia seeds, almond milk, vanilla extract, and honey (if desired).
2. Cover and refrigerate for at least 2 hours or overnight, stirring occasionally until it thickens.
3. Serve topped with fresh berries.

Nutritional Information (per serving):

Calories: 150 Carbohydrates: 15g Fiber: 10g Protein: 4g

APPETIZERS AND SNACKS

6. Hummus and Veggie Platter

Servings: 4

Prep Time: 10 minutes

Ingredients:

- 1 cup hummus (homemade or store-bought)
- Assorted fresh vegetables (carrots, cucumbers, bell peppers, cherry tomatoes)
- 1 tablespoon olive oil
- Salt and pepper to taste

Instructions:

1. Wash and slice the fresh vegetables into sticks or bite-sized pieces.
2. Arrange the veggies on a platter.
3. Serve with hummus for dipping.

Nutritional Information (per serving):

Calories: 150 Carbohydrates: 15g Fiber: 5g Protein: 6g

7. Baked Sweet Potato Fries

Servings: 2

Cook Time: 30 minutes

Ingredients:

- 2 medium sweet potatoes, cut into fries
- 1 tablespoon olive oil
- 1/2 teaspoon paprika
- Salt and pepper to taste

Instructions:

1. Preheat the oven to 425°F (220°C).
2. In a bowl, toss the sweet potato fries with olive oil, paprika, salt, and pepper until well coated.
3. Spread the fries in a single layer on a baking sheet.
4. Bake for 25-30 minutes, flipping once halfway through, until fries are crispy.
5. Serve hot.

Nutritional Information (per serving):

Calories: 180 Carbohydrates: 30g Fiber: 5g Protein: 2g

8. Greek Yogurt and Cucumber Dip

Servings: 4

Prep Time: 10 minutes

Ingredients:

- 1 cup Greek yogurt (unsweetened)
- 1 cucumber, finely grated and drained
- 2 cloves garlic, minced
- 1 tablespoon fresh dill, chopped
- Salt and pepper to taste
- Whole-grain pita bread or cucumber slices for dipping

Instructions:

1. In a bowl, combine Greek yogurt, grated cucumber, minced garlic, and chopped dill.
2. Season with salt and pepper to taste.
3. Chill in the refrigerator for 30 minutes before serving.
4. Serve with whole-grain pita bread or cucumber slices.

Nutritional Information (per serving):

Calories: 80 Carbohydrates: 6g Fiber: 1g Protein: 6g

9. Roasted Chickpeas

Servings: 4

Cook Time: 35 minutes

Ingredients:

- 2 cans (15 oz each) chickpeas, drained and rinsed
- 2 tablespoons olive oil
- 1 teaspoon ground cumin
- 1/2 teaspoon smoked paprika
- Salt and pepper to taste

Instructions:

1. Preheat the oven to 400°F (200°C).
2. In a bowl, toss chickpeas with olive oil, ground cumin, smoked paprika, salt, and pepper until evenly coated.
3. Spread chickpeas on a baking sheet.
4. Roast for 30-35 minutes, shaking the pan occasionally, until chickpeas are crispy.
5. Allow to cool before serving.

Nutritional Information (per serving):

Calories: 160 Carbohydrates: 20g Fiber: 6g Protein: 7g

MAIN COURSES

10.   Quinoa and Black Bean Salad

Servings: 4

Cook Time: 25 minutes

Ingredients:

- 1 cup quinoa
- 2 cups water
- 1 can (15 oz) black beans, drained and rinsed
- 1 cup diced bell peppers (red, yellow, green)
- 1/2 cup diced red onion
- 1/2 cup fresh cilantro, chopped
- Juice of 2 limes
- 2 tablespoons olive oil
- Salt and pepper to taste
- Avocado slices for garnish (optional)

Instructions:

1. Rinse quinoa thoroughly under cold water. In a saucepan, combine quinoa and water. Bring to a boil, then reduce heat to low, cover, and simmer for 15-20 minutes, or until quinoa is cooked and water is absorbed.

2. In a large bowl, combine cooked quinoa, black beans, diced bell peppers, red onion, and cilantro.

3. In a small bowl, whisk together lime juice and olive oil. Season with salt and pepper.

4. Pour the dressing over the salad and toss to combine.

5. Serve as a main dish or side, garnished with avocado slices if desired.

Nutritional Information (per serving):

Calories: 320 Carbohydrates: 53g Fiber: 11g Protein: 12g

11.   Baked Salmon with Asparagus

Servings: 2

Cook Time: 25 minutes

Ingredients:

- 2 salmon fillets (6 oz each)
- 1 bunch asparagus, trimmed
- 2 tablespoons olive oil
- 2 cloves garlic, minced
- 1 lemon, sliced
- Salt and pepper to taste

Instructions:

1. Preheat the oven to 400°F (200°C).
2. Place the salmon fillets and asparagus on a baking sheet.
3. Drizzle olive oil over the salmon and asparagus. Sprinkle minced garlic, salt, and pepper evenly.
4. Place lemon slices on top of the salmon.
5. Bake for 15-20 minutes or until the salmon flakes easily with a fork. Serve hot.

Nutritional Information (per serving):

Calories: 350 Carbohydrates: 9g Fiber: 4g Protein: 30g

12.   Lentil and Vegetable Stir-Fry

Servings: 4

Cook Time: 30 minutes

Ingredients:

- 1 cup green or brown lentils, cooked
- 2 cups mixed vegetables (broccoli, bell peppers, snap peas)
- 2 tablespoons low-sodium soy sauce
- 1 tablespoon olive oil
- 2 cloves garlic, minced
- 1 teaspoon ginger, minced

Instructions:

1. In a large skillet, heat olive oil over medium-high heat. Add minced garlic and ginger, and sauté for 1-2 minutes until fragrant.
2. Add the mixed vegetables and stir-fry for 5-7 minutes until they are tender-crisp.
3. Add cooked lentils and soy sauce to the skillet. Stir-fry for an additional 3-4 minutes until everything is heated through.

Nutritional Information (per serving):

Calories: 250 Carbohydrates: 38g Fiber: 10g Protein: 15g

13.   Spaghetti Squash with Pesto

Servings: 4

Cook Time: 40 minutes

Ingredients:

- 1 medium spaghetti squash
- 1 cup cherry tomatoes, halved
- 1/4 cup pesto sauce (store-bought or homemade)
- 2 tablespoons grated Parmesan cheese

Instructions:

1. Preheat the oven to 375°F (190°C).
2. Cut the spaghetti squash in half lengthwise, scoop out the seeds, and place it cut-side down on a baking sheet. Bake for 30-35 minutes or until tender.
3. Use a fork to scrape the flesh of the cooked squash into "spaghetti" strands.
4. In a large bowl, toss the spaghetti squash with cherry tomatoes and pesto sauce.
5. Sprinkle with grated Parmesan cheese

Nutritional Information (per serving):

Calories: 180 Carbohydrates: 20g Fiber: 4g Protein: 4g

14.   Chicken and Vegetable Stir-Fry

Servings: 4

Cook Time: 25 minutes

Ingredients:

- 1 lb boneless, skinless chicken breast, cut into strips
- 2 cups mixed vegetables (broccoli, bell peppers, carrots)
- 2 tablespoons low-sodium soy sauce
- 1 tablespoon olive oil
- 2 cloves garlic, minced
- 1 teaspoon ginger, minced

Instructions:

1. In a large skillet, heat olive oil over medium-high heat. Add minced garlic and ginger, and sauté for 1-2 minutes until fragrant.
2. Add the chicken strips and cook until no longer pink, about 5-7 minutes.
3. Add the mixed vegetables and stir-fry for an additional 5-7 minutes until they are tender-crisp.
4. Pour in the soy sauce and stir to combine. Serve hot.

Nutritional Information (per serving):

Calories: 220 Carbohydrates: 10g Fiber: 3g Protein: 25g

15.   Eggplant Parmesan

Servings: 4

Cook Time: 45 minutes

Ingredients:

- 2 medium-sized eggplants, sliced into 1/4-inch rounds
- 2 cups marinara sauce (look for low sugar content)
- 2 cups part-skim mozzarella cheese, shredded
- 1/2 cup grated Parmesan cheese
- 1/2 cup whole wheat breadcrumbs
- 2 tablespoons olive oil
- 2 eggs, beaten
- Fresh basil leaves for garnish
- Salt and pepper to taste

Instructions:

1. Preheat the oven to 375°F (190°C).
2. Place eggplant slices on a baking sheet, brush with olive oil, and season with salt and pepper. Bake for 15-20 minutes until tender.
3. In a shallow dish, combine breadcrumbs with grated Parmesan cheese.
4. Dip each eggplant slice in beaten egg, then coat with the breadcrumb mixture.

5. In a greased baking dish, spread a thin layer of marinara sauce. Place a layer of breaded eggplant slices on top.

6. Repeat layers, finishing with a layer of marinara sauce on top.

7. Sprinkle mozzarella cheese over the top.

8. Bake for 25-30 minutes or until the cheese is bubbly and golden.

9. Garnish with fresh basil leaves before serving.

Nutritional Information (per serving):

Calories: 350 Carbohydrates: 25g Fiber: 8g Protein: 18g

CONCLUSION

As we reach the final pages of this comprehensive guide to Low Glycemic Index (GI) Foods, I hope you're feeling not just informed, but also inspired and empowered. The journey we've embarked upon together has been one of discovery, transformation, and the celebration of healthier choices. But remember, this journey doesn't end here; it's just the beginning.

Your newfound knowledge of the Glycemic Index, the art of making low GI food choices, and the culinary skills you've developed along the way are invaluable assets on your path to better health. They are tools that will serve you well, helping you manage your blood sugar levels, achieve and maintain a healthy weight, and reduce your risk of chronic diseases.

As you continue to embrace low GI eating in your daily life, I encourage you to be mindful of the profound impact it can have not only on your physical health but also on your overall well-being. Celebrate the joy of nourishing your body with foods that provide lasting energy and vitality. Relish the flavors of whole, unprocessed ingredients that support your health and vitality.

But most importantly, never underestimate the power of feedback. Your experiences, your challenges, and your successes are all valuable sources of insight, not only for yourself but for others on their own journeys. Share your stories, your favorite low GI recipes, and your tips for making this lifestyle sustainable with friends, family, and within the broader community.

Your feedback is not only welcome; it's essential. It helps me and others in the field of nutrition continue to refine our approach, develop new strategies, and ensure that the knowledge we share remains up-to-date and relevant. Together, we can create a ripple effect of positive change, inspiring more individuals to embrace low GI eating and experience the benefits for themselves.

As you go forth from this book, remember that your health is your most valuable asset, and the choices you make each day can either nurture or challenge it. I hope this guide has equipped you with the tools and insights you need to make choices that promote your well-being and help you lead a healthier, more vibrant life.

Thank you for joining me on this journey through the world of Low Glycemic Index Foods. Your commitment to your health and the health of those around you is a powerful force for positive change. I look forward to hearing about your successes, your challenges, and the delicious low GI meals you create.

Printed in Dunstable, United Kingdom